Funakoshi Gichin & Funakoshi Yoshitaka:
Two Karate Masters

Funakoshi Gichin

Funakoshi Yoshitaka:

Two Karate Masters

Henning Wittwer

Disclaimer: The author and the publisher are not responsible for any injury (mental and/or physical) which may arise from the misuse of techniques illustrated or expressed in this book. You have to consult a physican before engaging in physical practise.

Impressum
Copyright: © 2015 Henning Wittwer.
All rights reserved.
ISBN 978-1517675240

Table of Contents

On Translation and Transcription

For the transcription of Japanese terms I roughly follow the Hepburn System, and for the transcription of Chinese words I use the Wade-Giles System. For Okinawan terms I follow Sakihara. Japanese and Chinese Names are given in the original order, i.e. the family name comes first. Square brackets in my translations indicate additional words by me.

Acknowledgements

While preparing this book I received valuable help. Antje Strehle provided many suggestions and representations on how to present my words in a clear way. Pierre Dobrzykowski did the necessary spell check and reworked the historic photographs. I would like to cordially thank them both.

Introduction

Today karate is the most widely used denotation for fighting arts which originate in the former island kingdom of Ryūkyū. In 1879 the core of this region became a part of the nation Japan. Since the beginning of the 20th century karate disseminated step by step on the Japanese main islands, Hawai‘i, in America and subsequently in the rest of the world.

The purpose of the book you are holding in your hands is to provide an introduction into the historical circumstances of this fighting art. What reads like an easy task is, in fact, not realizable without problems. First of all it is necessary to understand that karate is not only a kind of physical activity, which serves as a means to self-protection, winning medals etc. depending on the individual objects. It developed in a particular cultural environment; it was compiled, influenced and transmitted by particular individuals; characteristic teachings and folklore adhere to it. Karate would not be karate without these aspects. Furthermore, together with the world-wide propagation of karate technical deepness as well as theoretical knowledge dwindled away.

One crucial reason for this loss of knowledge is unsatisfactory language ability. The majority of old sources on karate are written in Japanese. More profound insights into the history and teachings of karate were and are reserved for persons, who are able to handle Japanese texts.

Notwithstanding Western karateka published many works on history and teachings of karate. In doing so they filled obvious knowledge gaps with a lot of goodwill and even more fantasy. In this way distorted ideas of the backgrounds of this fighting art evolved in the non-Japanese-speaking hemisphere in the last decades. However, in the Japanese-speaking hemisphere, too, statements regarding the history and teachings were and are spread frequently without examination.

Other reasons can be found in the political calculus, the personal interests or, for example, the business acumen of the conveyors of knowledge. Karate was and is a source of income for several persons. In order to optimize their profit, for these persons it may be necessary to use the conceptions of their respective customers (the karate students) as orientation. Sometimes manners of representation or contents of practise do not correspond to the personal interest or the supposed standing of a karate adept. Offhand he adjusts them. Also the political environment, be it small or wide, of karate practitioners may affect the actions of karate practitioner in some cases. Through all these points deliberately brought about changes in theory and/or practice of the karate of a teacher are possible.

Among the **misinformation** regarding karate which emerge again and again we find the following ones:

- Karate was developed in monasteries by weak monks, who somehow had to defend themselves.

- Karate is based upon Buddhist teachings like, for example, those of *zen* sects.

- Karate is based upon ancient Chinese breathing exercises and *ch'i* training.

- Karate was developed by poor peasants, who were not allowed to carry any weapons, in order to defend themselves against malicious occupants.

- Karate was/is an exclusive weaponless fighting art.

How can such misinformation be evaded, and how can the loss of knowledge be counteracted? For that, in my opinion, the access to Japanese sources takes the first position. In order to make them accessible to English readers they should be translated as close to the original text as possible. Thereby the reader not only gets a sense for the author's choice of words and manner of expression. But it is also easier to avoid or at least to reduce distortions or even alterations of content, made possible through text editing or more freely done interpretations. Of course, the disadvantage of this approach is the sometimes limited reading flow of such a translation that sticks close to the text.

Unquestionably, audience should be given to earlier adepts, for it is them who actually embodied karate. At any rate it should not be done uncritically. They can hardly competently judge historical circumstances of a more distant past, either, for example. Among other things it is necessary therefore to refer to general history books and additional sources for comparison.

Karate, the fighting art of Ryūkyū, was not transmitted in organised schools. A karate adept passed on his knowledge by means of very personal tuition to, in most cases, only a small number of selected students. Partially some of these students were able to learn from one or even more other adepts. Now, if one of these students for his part decided to admit and instruct one or more students, he passed on the knowledge and skills acquired by him.

So, if we want to track the historical development of karate we always view individual persons. We are concerned with a person himself or herself, with his or her teacher or teachers as well as his or her student or students. In this way **lines of transmission** come to light. These lines of transmission show the path a certain fighting art took while transmitted from person A to person B, and from person B to person C etc. Besides they show what fighting art contents exactly were conveyed and what contentwise developments a fighting art ran through.

In this book the focus of attention is the biographies of two karate teachers. It is a matter of a remarkable father and son team:

- **Funakoshi Gichin** 船越義珍 (1868–1957), who bore the pen name **"Pine Wave"** (Shōtō 松濤). Originally his family name was written with these characters: 富名腰.

- **Funakoshi Yoshitaka** 船越義豪 (1906–1945), who was given the nickname **"Devil of the Funakoshi *dōjō"*** (*Funakoshi-Dōjō no Oni* 船越道場の鬼). In the beginning his name, using the same characters, was read "Gigō". On mainland Japan the native Japanese reading "Yoshitaka" was used more widely.

Funakoshi Gichin (left) and Funakoshi Yoshitaka (right).

Connected to the name Funakoshi is the designation of a karate current which belongs to the widest disseminated and best known karate currents globally – Shōtōkan-ryū. In 1937 the

"Asahi Newspaper Publishing Company Okinawa" published a short summary on Funakoshi's life and work in its book "Record upon Human Affairs of Okinawa Prefecture". This summary shall afford us a first small insight (10, p. 318):

Karate Teacher
Funakoshi Gichin
29 Yumi-chō
Hongō-ku, Tōkyō-shi
[東京市本郷区弓町二九]

Being a national treasure possessed by Okinawa, our Mister Funakoshi Gichin [富名腰義珍] is a personality in the Imperial capital [Tōkyō] we can be proud of. Mister [Funakoshi] stems from the town of Shuri. For many years he was in the world of education of our prefecture [Okinawa]. In the year of Taishō 11 [1922] he participated in the "First Physical Education Exhibition"[1], [which was] organized by the Ministry of Education and the Arts[2]. This matter formed the beginning of him performing forms of karate[3]. In the world of the fighting ways [*budō* 武道] he was recognized and he went up to the capital [Tōkyō]. Opening a *dōjō*, he devoted himself to the dissemination and development of karate-dō. With that [he is occupied] until today.

---

[1] *Daiikkai Taiiku Tenrankai* 第一回休育展覧会.

[2] *Monbushō* 文部省.

[3] In this text karate is written with the characters for "empty hand", 空手.

Now the capital is the place where every institution of higher education shows the establishment of karate clubs. They disseminate and fathom out this way[4]. This is completely the result of Mister [Funakoshi's] endeavours and efforts[5]. And [so] it is also ascribed to his personality.

At present he is simultaneously the karate teacher [*shihan* 師範] of the Keiō University, the Waseda University, the Takushoku University, the Japan Medical College, the First Higher School, the Matsuzaka department store etc. In the world of the fighting ways of the imperial capital his good reputation is increasing. Besides Mister [Funakoshi] is not only a fighting artist. He calls himself [by the pen name] "Pine Wave", and he is good at Chinese poems. He is versed in *zen* writings and military science [*heigaku* 兵学]. He is a master [*meijin* 名人], who achieved the so-called state of unity of fist, *zen*, poetry and writing.

So, as seen from the perspective of Okinawa Prefecture Funakoshi Gichin was a person the inhabitants of Okinawa could be proud of. We learn that he moved from Okinawa to Tōkyō in 1922 and successfully disseminated and taught karate there.

Before we immerse in the subject on the following pages, still a few condensed remarks are

---

[4] The way of karate is meant.
[5] Translated more literally: "vehement fights".

appropriate. History in general is composed of rather dry data and facts on the one hand. They quasi shape its skeleton. On the other hand it also is composed of many anecdotes, narrations and pictures which are intertwined with the data and facts. They animate history.

Keeping this point in mind, in the fourth part of this book I introduce a timetable which prosaically and briefly points out some essential events regarding the Funakoshi line. I created it on the basis of my previous explorations. In the second part I present my complete translation of a biography about "Father and Son Funakoshi" which was composed in Japanese still during Funakoshi Gichin's lifetime. In the third part it is followed by a small photo collection which is intended to give a pictorial impression of the Funakoshis and their life with karate.

The biography about "Father and Son Funakoshi" was compiled by a direct student of the two Funakoshis. It contains historical events, and anecdotal narrations taken from their lives. Moreover therein interweaved are brief explanations on technical contents and the teachings of the karate of these adepts. To the biography I give explanatory footnotes and subsequently add a few annotations on the translation.

Father and Son Funakoshi
Togawa Yukio

One

"Gō'" – accompanied by an uncanny sound similar to the roaring of the sea a storm wind mingled with rain, which tied off the breath, started to thresh from the dark heaven. Branches broken off from trees, sand and small stones ached by flying [around with the hooting sound] *byū, byū*.

Since it is called the "Isle of Typhoons"[6] the violence of the rain storms that came to attack Okinawa surpassed the imagination. At any house, the ridges of the roofs of the houses[7], which were prepared for this single moment, have been constructed flat and solid. They strengthen the roofs with mortar and surround [their houses] with high stonewalls of one *jō* [ca. 3.03 meters height]. Nevertheless falling in with a typhoon whose momentary wind speed exceeded fifty meters [per second] [all] houses in the whole town of Shuri[8] whiningly screamed more and more: "*Hii, hii*". All people supressed their breath

---

[6] *Taifū no Shima* 颱風の島.

[7] Togawa gives the rendering *yā* for "house" at this place. *Yā* is an Okinawan term for "house".

[8] 首里. In the language of Okinawa this town is called "Shui", or "Sui". Shuri was the royal capital during the time of the Ryūkyū Kingdom (1429–1879). Today Shuri is part of the town of Naha 那覇. Naha is located in the southwest of the island of Okinawa and is the capital city of Okinawa Prefecture.

inside their houses, and prayed that the typhoon may pass through as fast as possible.

However, said "all..." was an error. Because in one corner of Yamagawa[9] village one man still offered resistance to the storm wind and held out on a roof.

A madman? – If there were people who saw that man, they certainly thought so. The man was a figure [dressed] with a loincloth [*shita-obi* 下帯]. It was that he, sinking down his hips [*koshi* 腰] at the top of the roof, where it was not easy to gain a foothold, stood [poorly] and, carrying a *tatami*[10] in both hands, opposed himself to the wind just from the front. He looked as if he had been already, driven by the strong wind, fallen down in rolling [fashion] from the roof. His powerful body was from the shoulders and from the back [on], not to mention the hands and feet, completely covered with dirt. Thickly dropping rain and sweat ran [down on him].

Seemingly the man had not yet turned twenty [years old][11], and he was an adolescent. He was a small figure of almost five *shaku* [ca. 1.52 meters]. However, the width of his body was big. With his swelling, towering up muscles like iron, it was an

---

[9] 山川. In the language of Okinawa this place is called "Yamagā". Today Yamagawa is a part of Naha. Togawa falsely uses the spelling 山河.

[10] 畳. *Tatami* are floor mats made of rice straw with measurements standardized for Japanese rooms.

[11] In Western counting this equals 19 years.

impression like a screen. He had the hair tied up like a wrestler[12]. From behind to the front in his hair-knot a small, silver hairpin shone, which showed that this man was of *shizoku*[13] descent. However, instead of such things his face, truly, was peculiar. It was under his hairs, which had been blown into a mess by the wind and rain and which he lost, [while] they stuck to his forehead. His face – small eyes, big forehead, wild like two deva[14] kings, all red, and a mouth clenched with an "*Un*"[15] – was filled with the power of his whole body. Putting both of his elbows at his flanks, tensing his breast, stretching his back and hips [*koshi*], the young man turned the *tatami* towards the wind and ardently held his ground. The most peculiar thing was from his hips downwards. Straddling both of his thighs, he stood in a form just as if he mounted a horse. If seeing people saw exactly this,[16] this was the way to stand unique to karate[17] called *naihanchi*.[18] It was that they understood that he was a *bushi* (in Okinawa

---

[12] *Rikishi* 力士.

[13] 士族. The term *shizoku* refers to families which had a status and a name in Ryūkyū kingdom.

[14] *Niō* 仁王. Meant are statues of deva kings, which usually stand by pairs in front of temple gates.

[15] Togawa uses the character 呍 for the groaning sound of *un*.

[16] I.e. people with a quick eye respectively people who have an eye for it.

[17] In this text karate is written with the characters for "empty hand", 空手.

[18] Togawa gives the rendering *naihanchi* and uses the characters 騎馬立, which can be read *kiba-dachi* in Japanese and signify "horse-rider stance". It remains unclear if Togawa wanted to express that the term *naihanchi* itself should be translated as "horse-rider stance".

persons learning karate were called *bushi*)[19] who used the storm night and learnt in view of certain death. The wind blew [against him] incessant, and even when it slacked it caused his body to fall down. However, the young man did not shrink back.

It is [sure] that this is a picture from the learning period of Funakoshi Gichin [富名腰義珍][20] (later he changed the family name to Funakoshi [船越]), exactly of this young man [just described], who later disseminated, lifted up the Okinawan tōdi[21] to Japanese karate[22].

Gichin was born on the tenth day of the eleventh month of the year Meiji 3 [1870] as the only son of a *shizoku* from the Yamagawa district of Shuri town, Okinawa[23].[24] Because he was a premature birth of seven months, his body was small and weak. Even his growth had been questioned. The physician said: "Seemingly it is that he will not maintain [his health] until ten years [of age][25]."

---

[19] Togawa himself explains in the bracket that in Okinawan language the term *bushi* 武士 signifies a karate adept.

[20] Here appears a misprint, because Togawa gives the old way of writing as 富名越 義珍, yet, it should be 富 名腰 義珍.

[21] 唐手. English: "Chinese hand" respectively "Chinese fighting art". Actually Togawa uses the Japanese rendering *tōde*. In order to avoid confusion I am using the correct Okinawan rendering *tōdi*.

[22] "Empty hand".

[23] Okinawa Shuri-shi Yamagawa-chō 沖縄首里市山川町. Again Togawa is using the wrong spelling 山河 for Yamagawa.

[24] In fact 1868 was Funakoshi's year of birth.

[25] In Western counting this equals 9 years.

"If it will not work anyhow..." – thinking so, his father Gisū [義枢] made his son to learn karate.

At that time the matter of karate was called simply "tī"[26] in Okinawa. Persons, who used *tī*[27], were regarded as *bushi*. However, it is not that every Okinawan could learn karate. That is to say the Shimazu clan had seized their weapons, and they had to learn the Okinawan fist method [*kenpō* 拳法] only, which developed since then, in strict secrecy.[28]

Gichin stepped into the gate of Asato Ankō[29] and a certain Itosu[30],[31] who were called master [*meijin* 名人] rather in Okinawa than [merely] in Shuri. I said "stepped into the gate", but because of the circumstances mentioned earlier neither there

---

[26] 手. Togawa gives no rendering. I am using the Okinawan rendering of this term.

[27] *Te o tsukau* 手を使う; in Okinawan: *Tī chikain*. "To use *tī*" was a wide-spread flourish in Okinawa. In modern karate terminology it means "doing a *kata*".

[28] In 1609 the Shimazu clan 島津藩 from Satsuma 薩摩, South-Japan, conquered the Ryūkyū Kingdom. In this connection the common misconception appeared that a weapons ban was imposed on the inhabitants of Ryūkyū. Yet, this conception has nothing to do with the historic reality (18, pp. 543).

[29] 安里安恒 (1828–1906). Asato learnt karate mainly from Matsumura Sōkon, a semi-legendary karate adept. I present a lot of information regarding the life and teachings of Asato in my book "Scouting Out The Historical Course Of Karate: Collected Essays".

[30] Itosu Ankō 糸洲安恒 (1831–1915). Itosu learnt karate from Gusukuma 城間 (dates unknown), Nagahama 長濱 (born ca. 1830), and Matsumura among others.

[31] I.e. he became their student.

were *dōjō* [32] nor were the students a predominance. By walking a way of one *ri* [ca. 4 kilometres] deep in the night or early in the morning, while paying attention that he [remained] unnoticed by the people, Gichin took up the teachings [of Asato and Itosu].[33]

Asato was a *tunchī*[34] (high-ranking *shizoku*). Not only was he excellent in karate, [but] also with the bow, and the horse, and moreover with the sabre. For example, on the occasion when Meiji came[35] and, following his former feudal lord[36], he went up into the capital [Tōkyō], he went out to the riding arena. It is said that one could see, that it was excellent when he practised [there]. He amazed the people in his environment: "This person there, who is that?" He was a person who did not show off, however, it is said that he said: "If they are real sabres[37], I cope with everybody." Therefore this person was a master. He worked as a fighting

---

[32] 道場. More complete is the term *budōjō* 武道場. It refers to an exercise hall, a training area used for a fighting art. Translated literally the term signifies "place of the way" respectively "place of the fighting way".

[33] I.e. the stretch of road between Funakoshi's place and his teacher's place was roughly 4 kilometres.

[34] 殿内. Asato held this rank by law of inheritance, and it belonged to the highest social classes in Ryūkyū.

[35] I.e. the time from 1868 on.

[36] The then king of Ryūkyū, Shō Tai 尚泰 (1843–1901), is meant. He has been deposed in 1879 and had to move to the Japanese capital of Tōkyō.

[37] In this case it is possible that sabres are meant literally. On the other hand it can also be a metaphor for a "serious" situation in a more general sense.

arts teacher[38] of the former feudal lord, and he was a real scholar [*gakusha* 学者]. His treatment was rather like a guest than like a subject [*kerai* 家来]. Itosu was his good friend. And it is said that this master Asato told the students always: "It seems that the fists of Itosu are real sabres." Therefore he, too, was nothing else but a master [*meijin*].

The special technique of Itosu was the matter to stab into the eye of an opponent with a single finger. When the person, who made an appointment with him for a fight, came and thrust, he lifted [the opponent's] arm, by rubbing it with a single finger – *sū'* – and stopped it at a place just one *sun* [ca. 3.03 centimetres] in front of his eye. [The opponent] was not able to avoid it. When they checked it afterwards, it is said, that the area rubbed by the finger, had become a bruise.[39]

Asato had a tall body and a meagre stature. His technique [*waza*] was fast. He absolutely did not allow the fist of his opponent to touch his body. However, Itosu was the complete counterpart; he had a small stature and was thick. His technique was heavy. As often as he [wanted] he allowed his opponent to thrust him and he was indifferent [to it].[40]

---

[38] *Budō shihan* 武道師範.

[39] Maybe this anecdote contains a misprint, and in fact it was Asato whose special technique is described.

[40] I.e. Itosu allowed impacts on his body.

"Only at the tip of the nose it does not work! Because only here I can't put power in! If it is anywhere else, wherever you thrust or kick, it is good."

As soon as [Itosu] drank *sake*, he talked in this way often. "Good!" – [regardless of] how often the young men thrust, he smiled. His power was strong and he did something like to show the crushing[41] of green bamboo. One evening he was attacked by several robbers on the street. Effortless he had knocked them down. There was one person[42] who spotted it with his [own] eyes. When [the person] informed Asato about this matter, Asato said: "I presume all the robbers did fall down, to lie turned round [on their bellies]."[43]

Being surprised the person who went to look at it asked: "Why do you know this?"

Then [Asato] related: "Regarding the falling down to the back, [while] thrust from the front, it is [so] because the technique does not work in such a manner. If it works in reality, they have to fall to the front. It is a matter of course that everybody bends down to the front if a person of the rank[44]

---

[41] "Crushing" refers here to "crushing with his hands".

[42] Possibly several persons could be meant, too.

[43] I.e. Asato supposes that all the robbers fell down to the front.

[44] "Rank" in this case does not refer to the modern karate ranks like *shodan* 初段, *nidan* 二段 etc., but is meant in a general way.

of Itosu thrusts. I presume they [can] not at all be saved.[45]"

Gichin was imparted [karate] by both of these teachers. By learning he seized the marrow of the shōrin-ryū [46] from Asato, and the secret transmissions of shōrei-ryū [47] from Itosu. The practise under both of the teachers was brutal. A single skill[48] was taught to him for three years. They did not go to the next one until they said: "Good!" In subsequent years Gichin related: "For ten years nothing but three *kata* were taught to me. Throughout every night I tried the same *kata* again and again. However, none of both teachers said to me: 'Good!' Around the time when the night becomes light and lighter [49] I returned [home] and researched it once more. Also during the period I slept, [deeply] dreaming, I swung my fists. Therefore I slept – even [after] I married – by separating the bed of my wife around four *shaku* [ca. 1.21 meters] [from my bed]."

Gichin's maternal grandfather was the sinologist[50] Oyadomari [親泊]. Therefore from the time of his

---

[45] I.e. they all will probably die.

[46] 昭林流. Shōrin-ryū means "style of the shining grove" in this case. Funakoshi used these characters in 1922, however, changed them later.

[47] 昭霊流. Shōrei-ryū means "style of the shining soul" in this case.

[48] *Waza* 業. Here a *kata* is probably meant.

[49] I.e. at daybreak.

[50] *Kangaku-sha* 漢学者. The term refers to a scholar whose subject is the so-called Chinese classics.

childhood he could learn sinology, compose Chinese poems etc.

He decided that he want to become a physician in the beginning. Therefore he entered the Training Institute for Physicians attached to the Prefectural Hospital[51]. And then he left the school[52] soon [prematurely]. The reason for that is hefty.

At that time Okinawa quarrelled, and it was split into the Stubbornness Party [*Ganko-tō* 頑固党] and the Enlightenment[53] Party [*Kaika-tō* 開化党]. These were no political parties. At the time when Meiji came and the hair-cutting dictation [*danpatsu-rei* 断髪令] was announced the old groups rejected the cutting off of the hair for everyone together. These groups were called the Stubbornness Party. Persons who did cut off the hair were called Enlightenment Party, and they were hostile to each other for every matter. Sometimes it was even that one saw blood. Gichin did belong to neither of the two [parties]. However, his father and mother were from the Stubbornness Party, which is why he continued with tying up the hair until he reached twenty years[54]. However, the matter of tying up the hair was not allowed at the school. Although he expressly entered the Training Institute, he could

---

[51] *Kenritsu Byōin Fuzoku no Ishi Kyōshūjo* 県立病院附属の医師教習所.
[52] The Training Institute for Physicians is meant.
[53] "Enlightenment" is meant in the sense of cultural renewal.
[54] In Western counting this equals 19 years.

do nothing but to leave the school empty-[handed].

Next he decided [to become] a teacher. He passed the qualification exam for elementary school teachers[55] (basic course for primary school teachers). However, here, too, his tied up hair became a problem. He, who stood loyal by his parents, knew about the error to struggle against the tides of time. On the spur of the moment he cut his hair. There is even an anecdote preserved [about that]. When he returned home, it is said, his father became angry: "Traitor!" And his mother ran from the backdoor to her parental home: "I don't want to see your face!"

Soon he was appointed to [become] an elementary school teacher at the elementary school in Naha[56]. In the port town of Naha the spirit of the people was wild by nature, and the power of the Stubbornness Party was strong. At the school it happened, that they seized one by one student who tied up the hair, and cut them their hair. For that they unconditionally needed Gichin, who was a *bushi*.

The two teachers, Asato and Itosu, permitted Gichin, who paid them a visit because of the transfer, to do it: "Whenever you taught *tī* already it became a good accomplishment. When you will go to Naha it is good that you disseminate the *shuri-te*."

---

[55] *Shōgakkō kundō* 小学校訓導.
[56] In the language of Okinawa this town is called "Nāfa".

The karate taught in Shuri was called *shuri-te*, and the style taught in Naha [was called] *naha-te*.[57] Regarding the technique [*waza*] on the part of Shuri it has been researched into the distance.[58]

Moving to Naha, Gichin followed the teaching profession for thirty years. Gichin, who received the instructions of the two teachers Asato and Itosu, not [only] persisted in the single point of the fighting art. Besides the sinology and Chinese poetry he was good at calligraphy and literature,

---

[57] *Shuri-te* 首里手 and *naha-te* 那覇手. The meanings of these terms in each instance are "hand from Shuri" respectively "fighting art from Shuri" and "hand from Naha" respectively "fighting art from Naha". In the language of Okinawa they are read *shui-di* and *nāfa-di*. The designations *shuri-te*, *naha-te* and *tomari-te* are quite recent. In October 1926 Kanō Jigorō 嘉納治五郎 (1860–1938), who compiled the Kōdōkan jūdō and who was a pioneer of physical education in Japan, received an invitation to Okinawa from the Okinawan branch of the "Japanese Association of Physical Education" as well as the "Okinawan Association of Jūdō *Yūdansha* ['black belts']". There among other things a karate demonstration was organised for him. On the occasion of this demonstration it was expressed that the term "karate" is unsightly. To have a counterproposal on the spot the terms *shuri-te*, *naha-te*, and *tomari-te* were invented (4, pp. 140). They have no historical roots, i.e. in older texts they are not mentioned. In the text Togawa gives the renderings *shuri-de* and *naha-de* which are a kind of a mixture of standard Japanese and Okinawan pronunciation. Since this anecdote took place many years before 1926 it is rather unlikely that Itosu and Asato actually used the terms *shuri-te* or *naha-te*.

[58] Probably Togawa means that in the *shuri-te* a great fighting distance was preferred.

at *haiku* [59] etc. And in the chrysanthemum cultivation he even had first-class appraisals in the prefecture [Okinawa].

Two

Speaking of Tsuji[60], up to the main island it was known more of Okinawa's street of songs with accompaniment [61] than Naha's [street of songs with accompaniment]. There was no plain world of prostitutes[62]. As a place of sociability of the Okinawans it had a character similar to [the red-light district] Yoshiwara[63] of the Edo time [1603–1867].

In the middle of the road that led to this place without night[64] there were lush and thick growing, big *gajimaru*[65] trees. The rumour arose that every

---

[59] 俳句. Japanese short poem consisting of 17 syllables (morae), which follow the scheme of 5 syllables – 7 syllables – 5 syllables.

[60] 辻. In the language of Okinawa this place is called "Chīji". Tsuji was a red-light district originally established in 1672. (18, p. 195) Today Tsuji belongs to the city of Naha.

[61] "Accompaniment" refers to an accompanying instrument, namely a stringed instrument.

[62] *Karyū-kai* 花柳界. Literally translated this term means "world of blossoms and willows". "Blossoms and willows" expresses beauty.

[63] 吉原. Translated Yoshiwara means roughly "field of luck", and it has been the only licensed red-light district of Edo (today: Tōkyō).

[64] I.e. Tsuji was a sleepless place.

[65] 榕樹. Togawa presents the *kanji* without pronunciation. The Okinawan name of this tree is *gajimaru*, its Latin name is *ficus microcarpa*, and its English name Chinese banyan. According to Sakihara it is banyan tree with small leaves.

night a street brawler, who was no street killer[66], appeared, who – under cover of this darkness[67] – waylaid and threw down brothel visitors by thrusting [them].

Persons, who were proud of their abilities, went out. However, it seems that the suspicious bloke was a rather skilful person[68]. It was that they all were thrust and kicked [by him], and injured themselves badly, and withdrew headless. Because he was no robber, he didn't rob things[69]. However, in order to get acquainted with his fists, [which] he forged by thrusting a *makiwara*[70], the danger of doing practical experiments was unavoidable.

One day Gichin received the request from the school principal:

"For the good of all [people] may I ask you, by any chance, to punish him?"

Since he had left Shuri he also neglected the practise [*keiko*] not even a single day. His fists

---

[66] The term translated by me as "street killer", *tsuji-giri* 辻斬, has the tenor that the murder is conducted using a cutting weapon like a Japanese sabre.

[67] The darkness created by the thick trees is meant in this case.

[68] Also in the sense of "experienced person".

[69] Also in the sense of "wares".

[70] 巻藁. Literally *makiwara* means "rolled straw". It is a matter of a straw bundle attached to a wooden post. A *makiwara* is used as utensil for striking and thrusting exercises.

were hard as a rock. At his elbows his one *sun* [ca. 3.03 centimetres] thick elbow callosities stood forth. However, concerning the display of karate, [in his case] there was really not a single time. Not only this: because of his hidden study even persons were rare, who knew about the matter that he is a master of karate.

"For the good of all, may I ..."

When he was besought in this way once, he couldn't say no.

By dressing like a brothel visitor at this evening, he strolled with the magnificent lights of Tsuji in his back.

The moon was beautiful. The *gajimaru* thicket got closer, big and pitch-black.

Close by the shadow of a tree Gichin halted his steps [shortly]. He observed it still, and as expected a sturdy man was cowering [there]. It was the posture of a test thrust. Provided that he went past in front with eyes not accustomed to the darkness, probably the right hand of the man would have extended and [Gichin] would have to swallow it into the side of his stomach.

With scuffing feet [*suri-ashi* 摺り足] Gichin moved forward to the flank of the man. There he had a posture [*kamae* 構え] without an opening.

Suddenly the man stood up and assumed a [fighting] posture. Yet, Gichin wasn't frightened[71]. Also his feet didn't stop. Two *shaku* [ca. 60.6 centimetres] in front of the man he stood opposite to him, and they did as if they [mutually] knocked together their noses.

The man was wordless; Gichin was wordless.

Now the man grasped one hand of Gichin. Being silent, Gichin allowed him to grasp it. The man pulled this hand [toward himself], and he allowed him to touch his right fist. The fist, seemingly considerable tempered, had hard *makiwara* callosities.

The man grinned as if he wanted to say: "How are they?" The white teeth shook in the darkness. Now it was Gichin's turn. Gichin gently grasped the right hand of the man, which had *makiwara* callosities, and held it in front of the face. It was a situation, where he could be seriously thrust [by the man] if he wished to thrust. Being silent, Gichin licked the *makiwara* callosities.

The figure of the man, who seemed to be flabbergasted, became cramped. He turned around and fled. Afterwards the man never turned up again.

---

[71] The verb translated by me as "be frightened" has the tenor "be surprised", too.

In the year Meiji 34 [1901] through the report of the school inspector Ogawa Shintarō[72] it happened that karate was included as a compulsory subject[73] in the Man's Normal School[74] of the prefecture [Okinawa] and the First Middle School[75]. Gichin was nominated formally as karate teacher. However, around this time karate was written [with the characters] 唐手[76], and one rendered it "tōdi"[77]. Concerning [the matter], that 唐手 became 空手, it is that Gichin gave it this name when he went to Tōkyō.[78]

It was a night duty evening. A pale young man staggered into the staffroom, asking for help. When he saw him, he had a nosebleed like

---

[72] 小川鋠太郎. Ogawa has been the principal of the aforementioned normal school from 1896 until 1899.

[73] *Seika* 止科. Ogawa's school inspection took place in October 1901. In 1902 karate was introduced as "teaching subject" into the normal school. Later, in 1905, it was included as a physical education "compulsory subject" into Okinawa prefecture's middle school. (12, p. 709)

[74] *Danshi Shihan-gakkō* 男子師範学校.

[75] *Dai-ichi Chūgakkō* 第一中学校.

[76] Translated these characters mean "Chinese hand" or "Chinese fighting art".

[77] In fact Togawa uses the Japanese rendering "tōde". As before, I use the Okinawan rendering "tōdi". It is possible to read these *kanji* as "karate", too.

[78] Gichin moved to Tōkyō in 1922. There he started to use the spelling 「空手」 gradually from 1929 on. Actually the spelling 「空手」 can be found in a paper handwritten in 1905 by Hanashiro Chōmo 花城長茂 (1869–1945), a student of Itosu. These characters can be translated as "empty hand" respectively "empty hands".

somebody who had received rather a lot of beating. He had his lips and eyelids slit.

While Gichin was taking care of him, he asked:

"What's the matter?"

And the young man said:

"I came under attack from a violent criminal."

Because he had no self-confidence in his proficiency, he got into this situation. It was that he requested: "Master, please teach me karate!"

The young man's name was Kanagusuku [金 城]. From the next day on with a burning heart he entered in the practise. Several years faded away and, step by step, he advanced. His shoulder muscles swelled, and they were called "two-storeyed shoulders". And it happened that among the students of Gichin he quarrelled about the first [or] second [place]. [79] Then rude and brutal manners became more frequent. Meanwhile it happened that rumours like "Because he drank *sake*, he quarrelled[80]" and so on reached Gichin's ears.

Sometime he said in front of Gichin:

---

[79] I.e. finally he belonged to the then two very best karate students of Funakoshi.
[80] Also: "scuffle".

"Master, please just test my proficiency! I expect that I did advance quite a bit already. Because by establishing a branch [of karate], I want to open a *dōjō*, and ..."

The background of these words could be regarded as self-encouragement: 'If I seriously engage the master then, I show him that I will win one out of three!'

"Good, let's go!"

Walking ahead in this way, Gichin went to the *dōjō*.

Taking their stands in a distance of two *ken* [ca. 3.60 metres] in the empty *dōjō* with not a living soul, the two persons stood opposite each other. Gichin, without change, stood with a dark blue serge stand-up collar uniform in a natural posture. It looked like he was full of absent-minded openings. The young man took off the jacket of his suit. Then he [moved] the left fist to the front, pulled the right fist to the hip, assumed a half-facing[81] posture bent to the front, and asked:

"Master, is it good so?"

"Mhm!" – Gichin nodded. Kanagusuku's facial expression became red visibly: "Well, if so, he is the master, and I will have no mercy with him!"

---

[81] More literal the term translated by me as "half-facing" means "half body".

Boiling with rage he began – hiss, hiss! – to advance with tripping steps.

One and a half *ken* [ca. 2.70 metres] ..., one *ken* [ca. 1.80 metres] ..., five *shaku* [ca. 1.52 metres] ...

"Kee'!"

With a scream[82], which resembled a beastly roar, Kanagusuku kicked the floor boards of the *dōjō*. The right fist of him, who flew in the air, dragged behind a white tail[83] from above until over Gichin's face. With his right foot and his left [foot] aiming at the chin and the breast of Gichin at this point in time, he started to kick. It was a sharp two step kick[84]. At this moment the body of Gichin, who stood as if he was absent-minded, opened largely to the right [side], and similar to lances bones and bones resounded[85]. The body of the young man flew away like a ball into the corner of the *dōjō*.

Gichin spoke to him with a gentle voice: "What's the matter?" He returned to the original natural posture, and his breathing was completely undisturbed. This was his appearance.

---

[82] *Kiai* 気合. In this case *kiai* refers to a fighting shout. A possible translation of this term is "right spirit", however, its meaning goes beyond a "scream".

[83] I.e. his fist moved so fast that it appeared blurred.

[84] *Nidan-geri* 二段蹴.

[85] I.e. the sound of the bones in this scene and the sound of fencing lances are comparable.

Holding his right arm as if it hurt, Kanagusuku – as tuckered out as he was – said:

"It doesn't work. I can't move my body."

Gichin said: "Does it hurt? Maybe the medicine[86] took effect a little bit too much. You have been battered; however, it doesn't hurt only you! Oh, I hear you are said to pride on your proficiency and to have rude and brutal manners, after you advanced a little!"

"Master, something like pride ..."

"No, I see it with my own eyes, too, you are pride. That you yourself suddenly go into a two steps kick against a skilful person is evidence of [the fact] that your study is not yet satisfactory. Think that the hands and feet of karate are real sabres! If you make a mistake, there is no life [for you]![87] The purpose of forging the technique [*waza* 技] is not to fell people. To improve oneself is the purpose! First of all forge your heart [*kokoro* 心] [more], than to forge your proficiency."

With tears [in his eyes] Kanagusuku threw himself down [before Funakoshi].

In the year Meiji 38 [1905] at the Manchurian Plain and the Sea of Japan the Japanese army got involved with the Russian army, and [therefore] the inland boiled and boiled. Okinawa, too, was no

---

[86] "Medicine" in the sense of "lesson" or "warning".
[87] I.e. he dies if he makes a mistake.

exception. Inspired by such a victory billow, the trend towards a rise of the fighting arts [*budō*] increased. Speaking with like-minded persons, Gichin went out to do public fighting art performances of karate in the Prefecture [Okinawa] in the years 38, 39 [1905–1906]. This was the beginning that karate, which started to develop as secret fighting art [*bu-jutsu*], was opened to the public. However, Gichin was dissatisfied with a mere introduction of karate. He thought: 'I have to introduce [88] karate, the Okinawan fighting way [*budō*], as physical education[89] karate far and wide in the world.' As a preliminary step he acted upon the Okinawan Medical Association[90]. Supported by it, he trained the children of the higher [school] class of Tomari's elementary school [91] in karate, and investigations on the changes of the state of health etc. were conducted.

In the year Meiji 43 [1910] he was delivered a certificate of appointment regarding the promotion to the [post of] principal of Kume Island's elementary school[92]. That is to say his diligence, called 'twenty-tree years of service without being absent and without accidents', was valued. However, he refused it. For, his grown old mother

---

[88] "Introduce" also in the sense of "present".

[89] *Taiiku* 体育.

[90] *Okinawa Ishikai* 沖縄医師会.

[91] *Tomari Shōgakkō* 泊小学校. Today Tomari 泊 belongs to the municipal area of Naha.

[92] *Kume-jima Shōgakkō* 久米島小学校. The island of Kume is located around 100 kilometres in the West of the island of Okinawa.

didn't like to dismiss him to far-off shores. Gichin, [who had] a profound childlike heart,[93] wanted to stay in Naha, in accordance with his mother's words. On this occasion he withdrew from the teacher's desk.[94] Then [together] with the like-minded Majikina Shōkō[95], who had a name as a historian [and] was the director of the Prefectural Library[96], and Sueyoshi Bakumonto[97], the editor-in-chief of the "Okinawa Times"[98], he organised the Okinawan Students Support Group[99]. This was a matter of doing it in such a way that they obtained school requisites directly from the mainland [Japan] manufacturer and distributed it cheaply at cost price among every middle school of the prefecture [Okinawa]. At that time he [together] with Mabuni[100], Motobu[101], Kyan[102],

---

[93] I.e. Gichin was loyal to his parents.

[94] I.e. he retired from the profession of a school teacher.

[95] Shōkō 笑古 (He, who smiles at the old) was his pseudonym. His actual name was Majikina Ankō 真境名安興 (1875–1933).

[96] *Kenritsu Toshokan* 県立図書館.

[97] 末吉友門冬 (1886–1924). Bakumonto was his pseudonym. His actual name was Ankyō 安恭.

[98] *Okinawa Taimusu* 沖縄タイムス.

[99] *Okinawa Gakusei Kōenkai* 沖縄学生後援会.

[100] Mabuni Kenwa 摩文仁賢和 (1889–1952). Mabuni learnt karate mainly from Itosu Ankō and Higaonna Kanryō 東恩納寛量 (1853–1915). He compiled the karate tradition of Shitō-ryū 糸東流. This name roughly translates as "Current of Itosu and Higaonna".

[101] In this case there are two possible individuals: Motobu Chōyū 本部朝勇 (1857–1928) and Motobu Chōki 本部朝基 (1870–1944). Motobu Chōyū probably learnt a family fighting tradition from his father. Besides he learnt from Matsumura Sōkon and Itosu. Motobu Chōki learnt karate from Itosu and Sakuma 佐久間 (dates unknown) among others. Togawa gives the rendering "Motobe" for this name.

Gusukuma[103] and a multitude of other gentlemen with the same predilection for karate established the "Okinawan Association of the Esteemed Fighting Art"[104], and he was nominated as teacher [*shihan*] and as chairman [*kaichō*]. Unifying *naha-te* and *shuri-te*, it decided tōdi [karate]. This time it did public fighting art performances in the prefecture [Okinawa], next time it went to Kyōto into the "Hall of Combative Virtues" [105] and introduced it [there]. He made his weight felt for this dissemination. In the third month of the year Taishō 10 [1921] His Imperial Highness, the crown prince, [106] enroute his trip to Europe

---

[102] Kyan Chōtoku 喜屋武朝徳 (1870–1945). Kyan learnt karate from Matsumura Sōkon and Oyadomari Kōkan 親泊興寛 (?–1905) among others. Togawa gives the rendering "Kiyabu" for this name.

[103] Gusukuma Shinpan 城間眞繁 (1891–1957). Gusukuma learnt karate mainly from Itosu.

[104] Okinawa Shōbukai 沖縄尚武会.

[105] Butoku-den 武徳殿. This hall was the central practise place of the "Great-Japan Association of Combative Virtues" (Dai Nippon Butokukai 大日本武徳会), which has been established in Kyōto in 1895. In the beginning its aims were besides the construction of the Butoku-den, the promotion, preservation and research of the fighting arts in general. In 1916 Funakoshi Gichin and Matayoshi Shinkō 又吉眞光 (1888–1947) did an official demonstration at Kyōto's Butoku-den. It is probable that Togawa refers to this demonstration in the text. Funakoshi performed the *kata* Kūshankū (Kankū), and Matayoshi demonstrated the use of the *tunfā* respectively *tonfā*, two short wooden sticks. (12, p. 517) Kyōto 京都 is located on the Japanese mainland in the southwest of Tōkyō.

[106] The crown prince is the later Shōwa emperor 昭和天皇, Hirohito 裕仁 (1901–1989). His trip to Europe took place from March until September 1921, and he visited Great Britain, France, Belgium, Holland and Italy.

condescended to do a side trip to Okinawa. On this occasion, doing a fighting art performance in the main hall of the Shuri Castle[107], he showed him [karate]. Therefore it happened, that step by step the "karate of Okinawa" became well-known in the centre [of Japan], too.

When Gichin heard that the "First Exhibition of Movement" [108] organized by the Ministry of Education and the Arts will be carried out in the fifth month of the year Taishō 11 [1922], he thought: "This is a favourable opportunity in order to introduce karate in the centre [of Japan]!" And [so] he went up to the capital [Tōkyō] at his own expense. The popularity of karate at the exhibition was exceptional. After the end of the exhibition he, who started to do preparations for the return home, received a visit from the painter Kosugi Misei (later: Hōan)[109].

Kosugi said: "I have been in Okinawa before already, right? Since that time it happened, that I have an interest in karate. However, in Tōkyō it was not possible [to practise karate], no matter what I did. Fortunately it is that you, Master, came up into the capital [Tōkyō]. Howsoever, may I ask you therefore possibly to teach us members

---

[107] Shuri-jō 首里城. In the Okinawan language it is called "Sui-gushiku" respectively "Shui-gushiku".

[108] *Daiikkai Undō Tenrankai* 第一回運動展覧会.

[109] 小杉未醒 (1881–1964). Misei is his first pseudonym, which means something like "He, who is not yet awake". His actual name is Kosugi Kunitarō 小杉国太郎. Subsequently he called himself "Liberated hermit" (Hōan 放庵). Togawa refers to this pseudonym in the parenthesises.

of the 'Tabata Poplar Club'[110], which is carried on by us, one or two methods on this occasion?"

Gichin thought: "This is a favourable opportunity!" [And also:] "In Okinawa karate is disseminated already; however, on the [Japanese] mainland it is still entirely undeveloped. To rise, to expand Okinawan karate up to Japanese karate: isn't this my destiny?" Seemingly both of his deceased teachers, Asato and Itosu, encouraged him: "What luck!"

Immediately Gichin sent a message home. He lived in the "Dormitory of the Clearness and the Right" [111] for students of Okinawa Prefecture, which was in Suidōbashi, Koishikawa[112]. He rented the lecture-hall and started with the practise. Although he was the teacher [*shihan*], he was also [occupied] there where a care-taker and garden overseer was called. Hearing a rumour, a person, who came to enter the school[113], [asked] the short servant[114], who was wiping the corridor:

"Is the Master there?"

"Well, who is the Master?"

---

[110] 田端ポプラ倶楽部 *Tabata Popura-Kurabu*. Tabata belongs to Tōkyō's northern district Kita-ku 北区.

[111] Meishō-juku 明止塾. It was completed in 1913.

[112] 小石川水道橋. Koishikawa is located in Bunkyō-ku 文京区, a central district of Tōkyō.

[113] In this case the karate instructions given by Funakoshi are meant.

[114] "Short" refers here to the size.

[The person thought:] "This servant there; he is a servant with a haughty way of talking."

"Of course it's Master Funakoshi of karate[115]."

"Ah, if [so], it's me!"

The new student was extraordinarily ashamed. Things like that happened often.

So he thought: "If this practise finishes, I return [home], I suppose; if that practise will be at an end, I return home, I suppose." Meanwhile [the number of] his students increased, and it happened that he had settled down eventually. However, he never dreamed that it would happen that this was a long farewell from Okinawa. One day Kosugi Hōan said:

"Master, if you return [home], there will be no person to ask for not comprehended places[116]. Therefore it would be good if you would leave behind some teaching script, and be kind enough to give it to us before [you leave]."

Gichin, too, was at the point where he already, for a long time, deeply felt the necessity for a teaching script. Therefore he did begin the composition of a karate teaching script. In the eleventh Month of that year [1922] he introduced the script called "Ryūkyū's Fist Method: The

---

[115] In this case Togawa is using the writing "Chinese hand", which can also be read *tōdi*.

[116] Also in the sense of "unknown places".

Chinese Hand"[117] to the public. This was the first book with regard to karate.

Meanwhile Gichin did public fighting art performances at the House Shō[118], at the "Building for Researching the Way"[119], at the Toyama School[120] and so on, and he made his weight felt for the dissemination [of karate].

There were two good advisors for Gichin, who had no acquaintance in Tōkyō. One of them was Jūdō's Kanō Jigorō, the other was Kendō's Nakayama Hakudō[121]. In fact both of them were famous fighting artists [*bujin* 武人]. Regarding the sentiments of warriors [*bushi*], one has to know real warriors [*bushi*]. Faced with the new fighting

---

[117] "Ryūkyū Kenpō. Karate" 「琉球拳法 唐手」. Strictly speaking this book was published on 25.11.1922. In 1994 a facsimile edition of this work came out.

[118] 尚家. In 1879 the king of Ryūkyū, Shō Tai, was deposed. He had to move from his Shuri Castle to a residence in Kōjimachi 麹町, in Tōkyō's central district Chiyoda-ku 千代田区. When Funakoshi came to Tōkyō Shō Shō 尚昌 (1888–1923), a grandson of Shō Tai, was the head of the House Shō.

[119] Kōdōkan 講道館. "Building" has also the nuances "school building" and "hall". This building was the headquarter of Kōdōkan Jūdō, which was compiled by Kanō Jigorō in Tōkyō. Since 1882 it had various locations. Funakoshi's demonstration took place in Shimo-Tomisaka 下富坂, Bunkyō-ku 文京区, Tōkyō.

[120] Complete: Military Toyama School (*Rikugun Toyama Gakkō* 陸軍戸山学校). It was established in 1873 and closed after World War II in 1945. Toyama 戸山 is located in Tōkyō's central district Shinjuku-ku 新宿区.

[121] 中山博道 (1873–1958). Togawa gives no rendering for his name. Usually there are two renderings, both using the same two *kanji*: Hakudō und Hiromichi.

art [*budō*] of karate, whose popularity began to increase, there were many fighting artists who were contemptuous this time, envious next time. Kanō and Nakayama, who were among them, [on the contrary] were not sparing with support for Gichin.

One day Kanō invited Gichin to the Kōdōkan and asked for explanations about karate in front of numerous high students. He [said]:

"Karate is a reasonable, magnificent fighting art [*budō*]! We can profit bulky by karate. We respect it and have to research it."

In outlines he reproved the prejudging [122] contempt. Moreover, Kanō said to Gichin once:

"It is that I want to try to establish a 'karate department' at the Kōdōkan, too. Would you be good enough to become its department director possibly?"

Even if it is said that the popularity begins to develop, in general [karate] is a fighting art [*budō*] not yet well-known. For the dissemination of this way[123] to join the large organisation of the Kōdōkan was also practical. Such a friendship of Kanō was felt by Gichin with deep gratitude. However, Gichin refused courteously. It was with conviction that he said:

---

[122] The phrase, which I translate as "prejudging" here, means literally "not liking uneaten things".
[123] I.e. karate.

"Karate-dō is a fighting way [*budō*] of the same rank as jūdō. It must never absorbed as a part[124] of jūdō."

It happened that the Okinawa Meishō-juku was rebuilt and [therefore] Gichin lost this practice place. At that time it was Nakayama Hakudō who let him, who was helpless, his own *dōjō* [saying]: "If it is for the dissemination of this way[125]." Gichin rented a house in Masago-chō, Koishikawa[126]. From there he went to Nakayama's *dōjō* "Building, wherein there is the Way"[127] and continued the practise.

Three

Around this time Yoshitaka, [who] was called "Devil of the Funakoshi *dōjō*"[128] came up to the capital [Tōkyō].

Gichin had three sons. The oldest son's name was Giei, the second son's [name was] Giyū. Yoshitaka was the third son.[129] Because of an injury the oldest son did not learn karate much, and [for] character [reasons] the second son [did not learn karate much]. Therefore he, who followed Gichin, was only Yoshitaka.

---

[124] "A part" may in this case certainly read as "karate department", too.
[125] I.e. karate.
[126] 小石川真砂町.
[127] Yūshinkan 有信館. "Building" has also the nuances "school building" and "hall".
[128] Funakoshi-*Dōjō no Oni* 船越道場の鬼.
[129] Giei 義英, Giyū 義雄, Yoshitaka 義豪.

Originally fathers did not teach their children fighting arts [*bu-jutsu*] in Okinawa. It was, because the love and the intimacy of the own parents created learning hindrances. The way of learning is a much, much colder matter.

Yoshitaka did not have a fixed teacher. Gichin, his father, asked both teachers Asato and Itosu for instruction by rendering the teachers courtesy. And it happened that [Gichin] did not alter their teachings and obeyed [130] them continuously. Thereby he was in stark contrast [to Yoshitaka]. It was not that he[131] constantly asked for instruction from the teacher here, from the teacher there. [Yoshitaka] endeavoured to recognize their outstanding points and their deficient points. Therefore for extraordinary [long] times he did [what's] called "observing practise"[132]. It is that he learnt only by studying through observation.

Then by bringing together their outstanding points, he completed a new karate and devoted himself to designing[133].

He related: "I did not learn karate from my father. If I am forced to say it, [then] I starred quietly at the fighting art performances done by my father."

---

[130] The verb translated by me as "obey" also has the tenor "defend".

[131] Yoshitaka is meant.

[132] *Mi-geiko* 見稽古. This way of practise consists of mere watching from the side, without joining the practise directly in a physical way.

[133] I.e. the designing of his karate.

High students commented [134] : "Regarding the fighting art performances of Master Gichin, if he is doing it a hundred times all hundred times are the same, and they are the accuracy itself. However, regarding the [performances] of Master Yoshitaka, if he is doing it a hundred times, all hundred times are different."

When he performed the *kata* Heian or the difficult *kata* Bassai, Tekki, Hangetsu, Jitte, Enpi, Gankaku, Jion [135] etc., Gichin's feet stepped exactly on the same spots every time he did fighting art performances. The single *kata* Tekki Shodan, which can be learnt if there are twenty minutes, was an achievement which he internalized in a space of time lasting three years. [136] These were *kata* from Asato, and those were *kata* from Itosu, too. Well, these were precise and incomparable forms of the Okinawan karate transmitted since olden [times] in the past. Yoshitaka's karate was different. His new interpretations and designs were put into [karate] by him. The thrusting fist,

---

[134] The verb translated by me as "comment" also has the tenor "criticize".

[135] Here Togawa is listing the names of the *kata* with the new spelling (*kanji*), chosen by Funakoshi Gichin in 1935 (or in the case of Tekki in 1941). However, at the same time Togawa gives the old names of the same *kata* as renderings. In the text I am using the renderings of the new names. The according *kanji* and meanings in the same order are: 平安 (Peace), 抜塞 (Removing Hindrances), 鉄騎 (Iron Rider), 半月 (Half-moon), 十手 (Ten Hands), 燕飛 (Swallow's Flight), 岩鶴 (Rock Crane), 慈恩 (Compassion and Mercy).

[136] I.e. its possible to learn the order of the movements of this *kata* in around 20 minutes, however, Funakoshi Gichin practised it for around three years.

the receiving arm – he researched the sense of its individual movements[137] anew. He changed the *kata* directly if he did not approved it and if he took his own idea to be right. Coldly he smiled at karate people who made the old *kata* into a golden rule[138]. When he performed a [certain] *kata* and performed it again, he made progress step by step. If that's so, perhaps one thinks: "This lout! He is conceited!" However, for him it was his confirmation. It was not so that he was satisfied with interpretations in his own way.

It was his goal to research [the question] what kind of change karate as physical education entails in the body during the period of growth. Therefore he learnt X-ray technology from Doctor T. of the Tōkyō Imperial University[139] immediately when he came up to the capital [Tōkyō]. Then he was employed as X-ray technician at the medical office of the Ministry of Education and the Arts[140].

Since the laboratory of Doctor T. was the location of the orthopaedics he began with the examination of bone fractures. Using X-rays he

---

[137] I.e. the individual movements of karate.
[138] *Kinka-gyokujō* 金科玉条, literally: "golden rule, jewel clause".
[139] Fusing three older schools, this oldest university of Japan was established in 1877 using Germany as prototype. Originally it was called simply "Imperial University", however, in 1897 its name was changed into "Tōkyō Imperial University". After World War II the reference to the Emperor was abolished, and it was called "University of Tōkyō". In the text Togawa uses the abbreviation *Tōdai* 東大.
[140] *Monbushō imushitsu* 文部省医務室.

examined human bodies with fractured bones. He researched how they get better if one starts to treat them [medically]. For this reason there was the necessity to break the bones of the [human] corpses placed at their disposal. With pleasure Yoshitaka undertook this responsibility. It is that he wanted to research in what way the thrusts and kicks of karate affect the human body. However, for that purpose he could not do experiments on live bodies. The research objectives of Doctor T. and Yoshitaka were different in each case, however, the methods did match.

Yoshitaka tried to thrust more than two hundred corpses from all angles. Then he realized the necessity to improve the "thrust" [141] taught in traditional karate.

He explained to the students: "Even if one thrusts straight, it only hurts. Human muscles [142] and bones are not that simple. If one doesn't thrust rising from below, or doesn't thrust diagonal downwards from above, they will not fracture!"

Based on such research in accordance with real combat he invented techniques [143] like the "rotating kick"[144], the "kicking into"[145] and so on,

---

[141] *Tsuki* 突き.

[142] The term translated by me as "muscle" can also mean "sinew".

[143] Literally: "hands".

[144] *Mawashi-geri* 廻し蹴り.

[145] *Kekomi* 蹴込み.

which were not in traditional karate [before]. By looking at the *maai*[146], he changed the "thrust", too, into a kind of jumping in, into a vehement method of thrusting which thrusts downward.

In the meantime they relocated [the *dōjō*] from Masago-chō to Yumi-chō, Koishikawa[147]. For the first time father and son Funakoshi possessed their own *dōjō*. Taking Gichin's pseudonym, the *dōjō* was called "Shōtōkan *Dōjō*"[148]. Even if it was called a *dōjō*, it was an out-of-doors *dōjō*, using the garden of an ordinary dwelling-house. Therefore the practise was broken off if it rained. And it is said that pines and lanterns [made] of stone stood here and there in the *dōjō*. Really, it was a strange *dōjō*. However, gradually there were more ardent students, too. Saigō Kichinosuke[149], father and son Asano Sōichirō[150] of

---

[146] 間合. I translate the term *maai* as "suitable distance". "Distance" refers in this case to the temporal and the spatial distance, as well as a mental free play; i.e. it also embraces a mental component.

[147] 小石川弓町.

[148] 松濤館道場. Translated "Shōtōkan" means "Building of the Pine Wave". "Building" has also the nuances "school building" and "hall". "Pine Wave" (Shōtō 松濤) was Funakoshi Gichin's pseudonym. In the text Togawa uses the simplified way of writing 松涛館, which was not used by Funakoshi himself.

[149] 西郷吉之助 (1906–1997). Saigō was a prominent member of the Japanese Upper House.

[150] 浅野総一郎 (1848–1930). He was called "Cement King of the Meiji [time]". His son's name is Asano Hachirō 浅野八郎. In the text Togawa gives these *kanji*: 浅野総八郎.

"Asano Cement"[151], two daughters of Takeuchi Zentarō[152] of "Takeuchi Safes"[153] etc. started to come to the practice. In the year Shōwa 3 [1928] they were invited by the Imperial Household Department[154] and did a fighting art performance in the "Building of Aiding the Serenity"[155] at the imperial court. Gichin's wish to transform "Okinawan karate" into "Japanese karate" was realized step by step. Each of the universities Keiō, Waseda, Business [college][156], Takushoku, Medical [college], the First Higher School, the Shōwa School of Medicine[157], the Matsuzaka department store[158], the Nisui society[159], etc. invited father and son Funakoshi as teachers [*shihan*]. At the University of Tōkyō, the Meiji, Nihon, Chūō Universities etc. there were also karate study-groups. On the twenty-ninth day of the first month of the year Shōwa 14 [1939] the new *dōjō*

---

[151] *Asano Semento* 浅野セメント. After World War II the company was renamed into Japan Cement (*Nihon Semento* 日本セメント).

[152] 竹内善太郎.

[153] *Takeuchi Kinko* 竹内金庫.

[154] *Kunaishō* 宮内省.

[155] Saineikan 濟寧館. The Saineikan was inaugurated on the area of the imperial palace in Tōkyō in 1883. Famous master teachers of the Japanese sabre and spear instructed at this practise place. Nakayama Hakudō, Funakoshi's acquaintance, was also active as teacher at the Saineikan. Nowadays it is used as practice place of the palace guards. In the text Togawa uses the simplified writing 済寧館.

[156] Today its name is Hitotsubashi University.

[157] Today its name is Shōwa University.

[158] *Matsuzakaya* 松坂屋. It is a Japanese department store chain steeped in tradition.

[159] Nisuikai 二水会.

Shōtōkan was completed in Zōshigaya, Toshima-ku[160]. It was a real *dōjō* wherein there was no longer the need to strike ones head against a garden lantern. The karate of the Shōtōkan current was not only taking the capital [Tōkyō] by storm. Branches [*shibu* 支部] were set up in Ōsaka[161], Toyama[162], on island groups[163] and so on.

In the meantime Gichin reached his seventieth birthday[164]. The practise already changed from the period of Gichin to the period of Yoshitaka.

Yoshitaka's karate, which was based on the fundament of science, fitted in with young students and the stratum of juveniles.

Step by step karate became famous and everywhere not a few persons appeared, who went around boasting greatly and talking big: "Karate is a fearsome fighting art." It is also that they astonished spectators by breaking a stack of four *bu* [ca. 1.2 centimetres thick] boards or

---

[160] 豊島区雑司ヶ谷. The town district Toshima-ku belongs to the eight central districts of Tōkyō, and it is located in Tōkyō's north-western area.

[161] 大阪. Today Ōsaka is the third-biggest city of Japan. It is located in the south-west of Tōkyō on the Japanese main island Honshū.

[162] 富山. Toyama is located in the north-west of Tōkyō.

[163] *Guntō* 群島. This term refers to islands like Amami 奄美, Okinawa etc.

[164] Following the usual European counting it would be the 69th birthday.

roofing tiles, what they demonstrated in the case of public fighting arts performances.

Gichin complained: "Regarding the breaking of boards or the breaking of roofing tiles, if one just steels the flat of the hand or the fist, it's a matter that everyone can do. To perform it as a show in order to quickly let [the spectators] understand the power of karate, is not karate itself. We have to do it quickly that we do public fighting arts performances without doing such a thing[165]."

One day in front of the Shōtōkan gate an unusual man emerged, who seemed to originate from a narrative called "Pigtail[166], moustache and black overcoat with family coat of arms".

At the reception he said [emphatically] old-fashioned: "I am Kishaba Chōhan[167], who has come from Okinawa. If Mister Funakoshi is at home, I would like to meet him."

It was not a familiar name. However, when it was a person, who came from the native place [Okinawa], [the person] was never simply turned down. When they tried to have a discussion there was big talk.

---

[165] I.e. Funakoshi wants karate demonstrations without tile breaking or board breaking.
[166] Here hair is meant which is tied up to the back of the head.
[167] 喜捨馬長範. Probably Togawa freely fabricated this name.

"I kill a cow with a single fist. With the *nukite*[168] (hand, which thrusts by closing the fingers and extends the flat of the hand) I have already stabbed into the belly of a pig and pulled out its entrails, too. If I seize jerkily, I tear off the meat, too, really!"

Gichin just smiled mischievously and did not become his opponent. [169] However, in contrast with his father, the vivacious Yoshitaka did not permit it.

"Interesting. I would like to ask you to tear off my shoulder muscles!"

He took off his practise dress [*keiko-gi* 稽古着] and pushed his right shoulder in front of Kishaba. Kishaba sharply glanced at Yoshitaka's muscular shoulder from the side and said:

"Hm, although you are young, it must not happen that you suffer injury! Because if the muscles are torn off, blood issues and one becomes a cripple!"

"Wonderful! May I die for the way [170]? Master Kishaba, please, do give it a try! Even if you tear off my muscles just a little bit, kneeling, I will ask you, Master, to accept me as one of your students! However, if you don't tear them off

---

[168] 貫手. Literally: "piercing hand". Togawa himself explains the term in the following parentheses.
[169] I.e. Gichin deliberately did not question the statements of Kishaba.
[170] I.e. „the way of karate".

please stop with such a big bragging! Because karate is a much more divine fighting art [*budō*]! Because it is not magic nor witchcraft."

Kishaba became very red and, taking off his *haori*[171], he stood up:

"What, if it is that I am bragging ... I hold you a lout, and if I am reserved, ... good! Such being the case ..."

Immediately Yoshitaka let him dance around, and precipitately he ran away. Whilst Yoshitaka's eyes followed the retreating figure, he smiled bitter:

"I presume that's not [what's] called 'overthrowing by amiability' ... However, such a thing poisons karate."

Yoshitaka's practise was by far more vehement compared to [the practise of] Gichin. One arm, which has been swept away just with his hand sabre[172] – bang! –, became numb. Afterwards it got a livid bruise.

During the practise time a black belt holder[173] asked him:

---

[171] 羽織. A *haori* is a Japanese overcoat which reaches down to the hips or thigs. It is a rather formal article of clothing.
[172] *Shutō* 手刀. Term for the pinkie side of the hand with more or less extended fingers.
[173] *Yūdansha* 有段者. Literally: "a person who has a step [*dan*]". At the Shōtōkan trainees with a *dan* got a black belt, i.e. this person was no newbie but someone who practised karate for some period already.

"Master, the person called Asato said: 'I don't let the fist of my student touch my body.' Yet, this is a legend, isn't it?"

In a carefree manner Yoshitaka said:

"No, that is perfectly true. Because by means of study as much is possible ..."

At the bottom of his heart the student [thought]:

"Well, how much is such a master able to do ...?"

Then he was on the point of thrusting Yoshitaka, who was finishing practise and just drawing back into the living room, with a "Ya'!" from behind. Jumping to the side nimbly and lightly, Yoshitaka turned round to the student and laughed:

"Try it and let's go, thrust me!"

So he brought together both of his hands by circling them behind his hips. "Damn!" – the student pursued him and thrusted. And Yoshitaka's body moved – *pa*! – backwards. His fist was five *sun* [circa 15.2 centimetres] in front of Yoshitaka's face. "This time sure!", he [thought] and he thrusted ... However, again there was a distance of five *sun*. When he stepped in three *shaku* [circa 91 centimetres], [Yoshitaka] moved backwards three *shaku*. When he jumped in four *shaku* [circa 1.21 metres], [Yoshitaka] moved backwards four *shaku*. His smiling face was always located five *sun* opposite the fist of the student.

Getting exhausted, the student asked:

"Master, it doesn't work. Why, I wounder?"

Yoshitaka explained:

"That's what is called *mikiri*[174] in the language of fighting artists [*budōka*] from former times! When you come and step in with *kiai*, it is that I quickly read[175] your strength[176]. Therefore if you come three *shaku*, I move backwards three *shaku* here, too. If you come five *shaku*, I move backwards five *shaku*. Even though you want to extend your fist beyond that, it does not extend beyond that. If you extend it [beyond that point] unreasonable, your body will collapse and fly frontward. If I want to move backwards, I go by adhering to the fist here. Do you understand?"

And he related:

"In short, karate is a fighting way at which one is tempering oneself extremely! Therefore [karate] is what is called 'outermost limit'. Formerly it happened that I let carry a man with a *sandan*[177] in kendō a bamboo sabre [*shinai* 竹刀], and

---

[174] 見切り. *Mikiri* can be translated as "the seeing of everything" or "see everything".
[175] "Read" in this case does not refer to the reading of a book etc., but the "reading" of one's opponent respectively the perceiving of the opponent's attacking energy.
[176] The term translated by me as "strength" also has the tenor "energy", and in the stricter sense it may mean "military strength" or "combative strength".
[177] 三段. Literally: "third step". It refers to a technical rank.

unarmed went into action against him here. At this time I was able to dive underneath the bamboo sabre, which came in to hit, and [I was able to] knock the bamboo sabre out of [his hands]. However, afterwards when I tried to let this man carry a wooden sabre [*bokken* 木剣] I was not exactly hit, yet, I did not jump in at all.[178] If it would have been a real sabre, I certainly would have been killed[179], I fear. Yet, so long as the skill [level] is not completely different it is not ill-considered to oppose a weapon carrying person with ones bare hands!"

The practise was vehement; however, he was extremely mild in the case of persons from outside. There is such an anecdote. One heavy raining evening he went back until the front of the *dōjō*, carrying an [opened] umbrella, when two drunken persons came from over there.

When he thought 'I want to get out of the way', his umbrella touched an umbrella of the others. It seemed that they were fellows who behaved badly when they were drunk.

The started to engage him [in a quarrel]:

"Hey! You scoundrel! Do you have esprit to go without greeting?"

---

[178] I.e. Yoshitaka avoided the wooden sabre attack; however, he did not approach in order to counterattack.
[179] "Kill" in this case refers to killing with a bladed weapon like the Japanese sabre.

"No, please excuse me!"

"Will you just apologise!? Damn it all, you will get into trouble with the Tiger of the XX gang![180]"

Speaking in this way, the drunken person folded up his umbrella and − bang! − beat up Yoshitaka with it. Yoshitaka, too, folded up his umbrella.

"With that it's better already, isn't it?"

This made the drunken person even more violent:

"You scoundrel!"

He had scarcely said that before he uninterruptedly beat up [Yoshitaka]. Yoshitaka silently suffered his beating. The rips of the umbrella broke apart and flew around. Then yet another started to beat him. After that [umbrella] was broken, too, both of them puffed and let their breath whistle. In the meantime [they said]:

"You are a cheeky scoundrel. Damn it all, confess your defeat, no!? With that we forgive you today; yet, from where are you scoundrel from?"

"Yes, I am from here ..."

Apparently the sign board "Japanese Karate *Dōjō*: Shōtōkan" did not catch their drunken eyes. When he returned back into the room, Yoshitaka smiled composed at his terrified spouse:

---

[180] Literally: "You will lick [taste] the Tiger of the XX gang!"

"Two hundred and twenty-seven [times] I have been beaten!"[181]

When his spouse opened the gate the next morning, there were two bottles of one *shō* [circa 1.8 litres] which had been secretly put down [there].

Four

The Pacific War [1941–1945] reached its final stage. One after another promising young man among the students fell in battle.

Yoshitaka [thought]: "For Gichin, who reached his evening of life, the matter will become really terrible." [Therefore] he made his father evacuate to his mother, who retired from Okinawa and was at the house of acquaintances in Kumamoto[182].

Apparently every night the city zones of Tōkyō trembled under the wings of the B-29[183] and were mowed down and burned. Notwithstanding Yoshitaka continued with the practise.

The last night came. It was the fourteenth day of the fourth month of the year Shōwa 20 [1945].

---

[181] I.e. Yoshitaka counted the strikes of the two drunken persons and altogether his total are 227 hits.

[182] 熊本. Kumamoto is a prefecture on the southernmost of the four Japanese main islands, Kyūshū.

[183] The complete name is "Boeing B-29 Superfortress". The B-29 is a long-range bomber with four engine-propellers, which was employed by the United States Army Air Forces against Japan since the summer of 1941.

Incendiary bombs did violent noises and fell down everywhere in the surroundings of the *dōjō*. The flames leapt up all at once, and there was nothing one could do, I suppose.

When Yoshitaka realized that it was aimless, he put a Japanese sabre into his air raid defence clothing and assembled the girls of the neighbourhood who had returned home.

"Is it all right with you? Please follow me! I certainly rescue you. Therefore [you have to pay attention] not to lose me ..."

Behind Yoshitaka in rows more than thirty just clothed persons, with the dress as it was[184] and with wholly pale faces[185], followed.

When they went on the street of the railway station Mejiro[186], at once they were criticized by a member of the "Protection and Fire-brigade Unit"[187]:

"Hello! Where are you going?"

Yoshitaka answered:

---

[184] I.e. besides their clothes the persons had nothing else.
[185] Literally: "really blue faces".
[186] 日白駅. The railway station Mejiro is located at Toshima-ku, where the Shōtōkan had been built, too.
[187] *Keibō-dan* 警防団. The "Protection and Fire-brigade Unit" was formed in 1939 in order to protect the Japanese civilian population in the case of air raids and catastrophes. Its members were civilians descended from diverse professions.

"Evacuating the women and children!"

The leader of the Protection and Fire-brigade Unit bawled at him:

"Idiot! Leaving one's district[188] and fleeing, what!? Do you mean this is the Japanese spirit[189]?"

Composed Yoshitaka said:

"It is the Japanese spirit. With these flames it will in no way work!"

And [he added]: "This large number of human life is more important than such a thing! Now during war one is excited. Therefore one takes such a thing as human life easy. Soon the time will come when you understand."

"What?! You, I am not allowed to let you through here! Return and protect them in your district! If it is the Japanese spirit you shall be able to do it! If you put out [the fire], all life is safe!"

"With bucket, duster[190] and Japanese spirit only one doesn't put out a chemical incendiary bomb. Regarding my people, they are women and children, at all events mixed with infants, too. How can I do that? Do evacuate them!"

---

[188] Also in the sense of "area of responsibility".
[189] *Yamato-damashii* 大和魂. "Spirit" has also the tenor of "soul" in this case.
[190] *Hataki* ハタキ. Such a duster consists of a long shaft. At the shaft's tip shreds of cloth are fixed.

"I am not allowed, go back!"

Suddenly the unit-leader thrusted Yoshitaka's chest and tottered.

"Fine! I no longer ask. I evacuate them by force!"

Yoshitaka said it so sharp, and flashing up draw his Japanese sabre out. [Confronted] with this energy, at the same time all members of the Protection and Fire-brigade Unit, who had surrounded him, dispersed – [screaming] "Wǎ!"

Yoshitaka shouted:

"So, let's go!"

There was nobody else who hindered them.

Soon the war defeat came. [191] Japanese, who [suffered] poverty and hunger and who had lost the proximity to the [Japanese] spirit, losing their will to live erred about like a shed hide.

At that time finally Yoshitaka rented a room in a multiple-family dwelling which was spared from the fire. Yoshitaka of all people did no assessments of how it will become better from now.

---

[191] Togawa refers to Japan's defeat in the Pacific War respectively in World War II in 1945. Formally Japan capitulated on 2nd September 1945.

One evening two high students [192] visited Yoshitaka. One of them said:

"I think Japan is beyond salvation. It is not to be expected that a nation, which has been defeated in this way and was completely deprived of its military preparation, will become a first rank nation in the world."

The other one contradicted:

"No, the point of military preparation may be beyond salvation. However, I am not saying that [Japan] will not become a first rank nation! If it is even possible to only leave over the spirit ... If it is even possible to only preserve securely the spirit of the Japanese ..."

The first man said:

"Yet, because it is still now, this spirit, too, grows stiffly anti-American. If still a little more [time] passes, it will be [like in the phrase] 'To let one envelop by a long thing' [193] , isn't it? If it will happen to ask for distributing articles of food, to receive clothes, immediately it will happen that we wag our tail at Mister America. Mister America utilizes no maladroit move like the Japanese army

---

[192] They are male karate students; however, Togawa does not reveal their names.

[193] *Nagai-mono niwa makarero* 長い物には捲かれろ. This is a Japanese saying. Some time or other a short thing allows the long thing to envelop it. I.e. it gives in and doesn't struggle against the long thing.

did in Nanking![194] We trap him into creeping up[195] from the side of Japan's daughters! At that time such a thing as the Japanese spirit had disappeared already!"

The other man said:

"I do not think that it's different! Actually perhaps such a phenomenon will emerge temporarily. It doesn't appear to me that the Japanese lose the spirit fundamentally. Therein are the existence and the sense of the fighting art [*budō*], aren't they? We have to [carefully] preserve the recovering spirit of the Japanese in the practice of karate, haven't we?"

For the first time Yoshitaka opened his mouth:

"I think the same way, too. Karate must have a big meaning by then. It is not such a thing like [mere] technique. It is certain that we cultivate[196] Japan's recovering spirit, which seems to has been lost, ... an invincible spirit, by studying karate-dō. Then we will do it this way. It is certain that it is the biggest assignment[197] of karate-dō in today's Japan."

---

[194] 南京. Since 1912 Nanking was the capital of the Republic of China. In 1937 the Japanese army did conquest Nanking and after that committed the "Nanking Massacre". In the text the speaker alludes to this incident.

[195] The verb translated by me as "creep up" can also be understood as "ingratiate" or "nuzzle against".

[196] The verb translated by me as "cultivate" has also the tenor "develop".

[197] Also: "biggest determination".

However, at that time a terrible disease demon was about to eat away Yoshitaka's body. Pulmonary gangrene — it causes that the lungs decay. It was an [even] more terrible, incurable disease than tuberculosis. Soon Yoshitaka went to deathbed.

New students shouted at the head [of his deathbed]:

"Master, please, live! Please, with the spirit of karate do not succumb to the disease demon!"

Yoshitaka showed a lonely smile in his pale face, which was emaciated and decayed. Apparently suffering, he said:

"Thank you! As far as I am let live, I will try to live!"

And these were Yoshitaka's last words:

"Even if I die, karate is preserved. If the spirit of karate is preserved once, then it is that the Japanese spirit is preserved. I have firm confidence in it."

His students rented the lecture-hall of the elementary school in Mejiro, which was spared from the flames, and devoted themselves to the practise. That what rose out of the burnt-out ruins was the sturdy germ of the Japanese spirit.

Ten years later ...

Eighty-eight years old[198] Gichin had come up into the capital [Tōkyō] and lived in Hayashi-chō, Koishikawa[199]. And it happened that he [obtained an inquiry] by the commander of the base of the American army in Kisarazu.[200] It said:

"I wish that you demonstrate karate for my subordinates."

Gichin asked the messenger:

"Is it[201] in Japanese style or in American style?"

The messenger asked a counter-question:

"I wonder what may be the meaning of the said [words]?"

Gichin said:

"The meaning is if you want to watch a Japanese fighting art [*budō*]? Or, I wonder, what do you want to watch by no means?"

The messenger replied:

---

[198] In Western counting this equals 87 years.
[199] 小石川林町.
[200] 木更津. The town of Kisarazu is located in the Tōkyō Bay. In 1936 in Kisarazu a military airbase was established. After World War II, between 1945 and 1956, this base was used as "Kisarazu Air Base" by the United States Air Force.
[201] I.e. the requested karate demonstration.

"Of course it is good in Japanese style."

Gichin demanded:

"If [so], please officially deliver up to me the invitation letter of the commander! Furthermore, I for my part will go wearing Japanese style formal clothes. Therefore I wish that you on your part will watch wearing official military uniform."

Soon the Japanese karate will become world-wide karate, I suppose. The dream of an old man, pictured in his youth, was about to come true far and wide, I suppose.

On that day the weather was magnificently clear[202]. Driven by car which picked him up, Gichin did [wear] Japanese style formal clothes, [namely] a black *haori* with family coat of arms, a silk[203] *hakama*[204] and white socks[205].

The car was driven on a long country road. When it came into the barrack gate, it was picked up by the commander in person. Then he escorted it, driving in a jeep.

---

[202] Translated by me as "clear weather" the expression literally means "clear Japan [weather]".

[203] *Sendai-hira* 仙台平. A special silk, which is produced in the Japanese town of Sendai 仙台, Miyagi 宮城 prefecture, since the end of the 17th century. This hand-woven silk cloth with vertical stripes was regarded as especial noble (15).

[204] 袴. A *hakama* is a Japanese style divided skirt for man.

[205] *Tabi* 足袋. One characteristic feature of a *tabi* is a division for the big toe, which separates it from the other toes.

It was a fresh, well-groomed base. Immediately Gichin saw a warrior memorial from the car window. This was a matter which was also consecrated as an aviator shrine [dating] from the time of the Kisarazu air force.

Gichin called:

"Ah! Please, just stop!"

The leading jeep of the commander drove ahead for a while, and [then] he realized that from behind the car of the teacher [Funakoshi] did not follow him.

The commander ordered the driver:

"Oh, car trouble! Return!"

The car of the teacher [Funakoshi] began, and [also] the car of his students stood still in front of the aviator shrine. Then the commander saw the figure of the old teacher, which very deeply bowed the head in front of the warrior memorial.

The commander jumped out of the jeep and went behind Gichin. And then he, too, rose [the hand] to salute[206] in respectful posture.[207]

---

[206] "Salute" refers to the military salute using a hand gesture.
[207] This text was published as one chapter in Togawa's book "Biographies of Fighting Arts Masters" (*Bugō Retsuden* 武豪列伝) on 10th December 1956.

Annotations on the Translation

Togawa Yukio 戸川幸夫, the author of this text, was born in the town of Saga 佐賀 on the southernmost of the four Japanese main islands on 15th April 1912. He entered the Higher School of Yamagata 山形 (today: Yamagata University), however, dropped out of college prematurely. Subsequently he started to work as a journalist for the "Day by Day Newspaper Tōkyō" (*Tōkyō Nichinichi Shinbun* 東京日日新聞). Since the 1950ies he published numerous books. In his adolescence he did practise jūdō and claims that he had "a little of self-confidence" in this field. In 1940 he started to practise karate under Funakoshi Gichin and Funakoshi Yoshitaka at the Shōtōkan. (5, p. 6) However, shortly after that he had to leave Tōkyō and did return only after one and a half years. (5, p. 10) Back in Tōkyō he began to help the Funakoshis with their karate teaching. When in 1958 the "Japanese Association of the Pine Wave for the Way of the Empty Hand" (Nihon Karate-dō Shōtōkai 日本空手道松濤會) was reorganized, Togawa assumed the position of one of its "advisors" (*komon* 顧問). (11, p. 21) He passed away on 1st May 2004.

Togawa does not mention which sources he used in order to produce his text. However, he wrote the text as a witness of a time period. He personally knew Funakoshi Gichin as well as Funakoshi Yoshitaka. Therefore a lot of information did probably flow directly from Funakoshi Gichin respectively Funakoshi Yoshitaka to Togawa. Another source he did use is the spouse of Funakoshi Yoshitaka. (5, p. 9) Furthermore he apparently resorted to some of Funakoshi's published works. For example Togawa's list of universities with karate clubs visited by Funakoshi as karate teacher (14, p. 203) resembles the list given by Funakoshi in his 1935 *Karate-dō Teaching Standard*. (2, p. 14) It is important to note that Funakoshi Gichin knew Togawa's text and even borrowed an excerpt of it in order to publish it almost word for word himself in his auto-biography.

Since Togawa wrote down these biographies from the point of view of a loyal student of both Funakoshis, of course, points regarded by him as possibly negative are lacking. To cast a perhaps "poor light" on his teachers supposedly was not his intention. Therefore it is not a too critical treatment. Furthermore he recounts some anecdotes in a rather dramatized way in order to create some entertainment value.

Nonetheless Togawa's text is of great historical value precisely because he wrote it down as witness of a time period and Funakoshi knew its content. Probably Funakoshi even assisted him in some way during the creation process. It contains various anecdotes from the life of the Funakoshis, from Asato and Itosu. Furthermore Togawa presents insights into the teachings of these adepts. Thereby it represents an important source for researching the karate of this line of transmission.

More generally it is notable that Togawa's text demonstrates how karate respectively karate practice has been used in order to regain the national pride lost because of the loss of the war in Japan's post-war years.

Photo Collection on Funakoshi Gichin and Funakoshi Yoshitaka

Group photo inside the Meishō-juku. Visible are a few weapons and practise utensils (*dōgu*) used in karate. In the centre of the picture Funakoshi Gichin is holding a *sai* (old, metal constabulary truncheon). Placed next to him are wodden sabres (*bokutō*) and a stick (*bō*). Placed in front of Gichin's free hand is a *makiwara*. At Gichin's other side is a characteristically formed stone weight called *chīshī*. In front of it is a pair of metal sandals. Among others we can see:

- Ōtsuka Hironori 大塚博紀 (1892–1982), front row, left on the outside
- Shimizu Toshiyuki 清水敏之 (1899–1979), front row, right on the outside
- Funakoshi Yoshitaka, second row, right on the outside behind Shimizu
- Katō Norio 加藤教雄, second row, right directly behind Gichin

Commemorative photo of the "Karate Research Association of the Tōkyō Imperial University" from October 1926. Funakoshi Gichin is the sixth person from the left in the second row.

Circa 1930 in a jūdō *dōjō* used by the "Karate Research Association of the Privat School Keiō" for its karate practise. In the photo we can see a *kumite* between Funakoshi Gichin and his student Obata Isao 小幡功 (1904–1976). Obata wields a stock (*bō*), which is received by Funakoshi with a *sai*.

Funakoshi Gichin (middle of the picture, front) while instructing members of the "Karate Research Association of the Privat School Keiō". The photo was taken around 1930. At this time the *kata* practised was still called Pinan. In 1935 Funakoshi published its new name: Heian.

Mabuni Kenwa 摩文仁賢和 (1889–1952) being a guest of Keiō university's karate club in April 1933. Standing behind him from left to right:

• Funakoshi Gichin
• Gima Shinkin 儀間真謹 (1896–1989)
• Ōtsuka Hironori
• Konishi Yasuhiro 小西康裕 (1893–1983)
• Mabuni Ken'ei 摩文仁賢榮 (born in 1918), the oldest son of Mabuni Kenwa

Excursion to Wakamatsu 若松 on the southernmost Japanese main island Kyūshū in the summer of 1935. Among others we can see:

• Funakoshi Yoshitaka, front row, fifth person from the left
• Egami Shigeru 江上茂 (1912–1981), front row, sixth person from the left
• Hironishi Motonobu 廣西元信 (1913–1999), middle row, fifth person from the left, directly behind Yoshitaka

Kumite at the Shōtōkan. Funakoshi Gichin (left) receives a *tsuki* of his student Saigō Kichinosuke 西郷吉之助 (1906–1997). The photo was taken circa 1939.

Circa 1940 at the Shōtōkan. In second row from left right sit among others:

- Katsushima Rokuichirō 葛島六一郎, forth person from the left
- Uemura Tsunejirō 植村常次郎 (1906–2002), after the Funakoshis the 3ʳᵈ teacher at the Shōtōkan
- Funakoshi Yoshitaka
- Funakoshi Gichin
- Noguchi Hiroshi 野口宏 (1910–2002)
- (unrecognizable)
- Hayashi Yoshiaki 林義明 (1907–1989) after the Funakoshis and Uemura the 4ᵗʰ teacher at the Shōtōkan
- Endō Kunio
- Egami Shigeru

Kumite at the Shōtōkan. Egami Shigeru counterattacks, after having received Funakoshi Yoshitaka's *tsuki*. The photo was taken in the early 1940ies.

Funakoshi Gichin with a movement from Kankū dai, his favourite *kata*. The photo was published in Funakoshi's 1935 "Teaching Standard of Karate-dō" 1935.

Funakoshi Yoshitaka with the same movement from Kankū dai inside the Shōtōkan. The photo was taken in the early 1940ies.

Funakoshi Gichin with a gesture from the *kata* Jitte. The photo was published in Funakoshi's 1935 "Teaching Standard of Karate-dō" 1935.

Funakoshi Yoshitaka with the same movement from Jitte inside the Shōtōkan. The photo was taken in the early 1940ies.

Funakoshi Yoshitaka performing a stick *kata*. Altogether five stick *kata* were introduced into the prepared but unfinished Shōtōkan curriculum.

In one corner of the Shōtōkan this egg-shaped punch bag was suspended. The photo shows Funakoshi Yoshitaka practising his *mawashi-geri*.

In front of the Shōtōkan this row of *makiwara* was erected. The photo shows Funakoshi Yoshitaka while practising at one of these *makiwara*.

Handshaking at Ōsaka railway station in the spring of 1948. In the foreground stand Mabuni Kenwa (left) and Funakoshi Gichin (right). In the background stand from left to right:

• Sakagami Ryūshō 坂上隆祥 (1915–1993), a student of Mabuni
• Obata Isao
• Nakayama Masatoshi 中山正敏 (1913–1987), a student of Funakoshi

Group photograph at the Kōdōkan in Tōkyō in 1952. Karate teachers around Funakoshi Gichin introduced American aviators of the Strategic Air Command into karate. From left to right we can see:

- Nakayama Masatoshi
- Noguchi Hiroshi
- Funakoshi Gichin
- Obata Isao
- Kubota Shōichi 久保田正一 (1917–1994)
- Emilio Bruno (born in 1914), the organizer of this training program

In September 1952 at a shintō shrine by the name of Tsurugaoka Hachiman-Gū 鶴岡八幡宮 in Kamakura 鎌倉 a karate consecration performance took place. Hachiman 八幡 is a Japanese god of war. In the front row stand from left to right among others:

• Obata Isao, fifth person from the left
• Funakoshi Gichin
• Kasuya Masahiro 粕谷眞洋 (1888–1969), an early student of Funakoshi and former chairman of Keiō university's karate club

Togawa Yukio 戸川幸夫 (1912–2004), the author of "Father and Son Funakoshi", in October 1953 (middle of the picture, above). In the front of the photo from left to right sit:

- Enomoto Eiji 榎本榮次
- Funakoshi Gichin
- Enomoto Masao 榎本正雄

Funakoshi giving a speech. This photo was published in the summer edition of the magazine "Karate-Dō. Monthly Edition" in 1956.

Example of a calligraphy by Funakoshi Gichin, which he signed with his pen name "Pine Wave" (Shōtō).

Its Sino-Japanese reading is: *Isshi dōjin*.

Translated this maxim means: **"One [and every] view the same benevolence."**

Interpreted more freely it means that one is friendly to all humans in the same way, or that one is friendly and benevolent in an impartial way.

In 1968 in Kamakura a monument for Funakoshi was erected, which can be viewed until today. The photo shows Henning Wittwer on a visit to this monument.

Timetable

YEAR	EVENT
1828	• Asato Ankō is born. Asato was the actual main teacher of Funakoshi.
1831	• Itosu Ankō is born. Itosu was the second main teacher of Funakoshi.
1835	• Shō Iku (1813–1847) becomes king of Ryūkyū.
1839	• In China the First Opium War (1839–1942) breaks out. The following social upheavals favour the dissemination of fighting arts.
1848	• Shō Tai (1843–1901) becomes king of Ryūkyū.
1867	• For the first time the spelling 「唐手」 ("Chinese hand") can be proved. It is used in a programme of performances.
1868	• Funakoshi Gichin is born.
1872	• The Ryūkyū Kingdom ends and Ryūkyū becomes a domain (*han*) of Japan.
1879	• The Japanese domain Ryūkyū becomes a Japanese prefecture (*ken*), namely Okinawa Prefecture. • The former king of Ryūkyū, Shō Tai, has to move to Tōkyō. Asato belongs to his staff in Tōkyō. • Itosu becomes a secretary at the Prefecture Administration. • Funakoshi begins with the karate practise.

1885	• Itosu retires from his job as secretary.
1887	• Funakoshi begins his career as school teacher.
1895	• Japan emerges victorious from the Sino-Japanese War (1894–1895). • The "Great-Japan Association of Combative Virtues" (Dai Nippon Butokukai) is founded in Kyōto.
1899	• The "Hall of Combative Virtues" (Butoku-den) is completed in Kyōto. It is used as a practise hall of the Butokukai.
1901	• Karate becomes established as a department of the gymnastics club of Shuri's elementary school. Itosu conducts the karate practice. • Shimoda Takeshi is born. Shimoda was Funakoshi's first teaching assistant (*shihan-dai*) in Tōkyō.
1902	• Karate is introduced as a teaching subject in Okinawa prefecture's normal school.
1904	• Itosu introduces the *kata* Pinan, which consists of five steps. Later Funakoshi called it Heian.

1905	• Japan emerges victorious from the Russo-Japanese War (1904–1905). • Karate becomes a compulsory subject at Okinawa prefecture's middle school. • For the first time the spelling 「空 手」 ("empty hand") can be proved. Hanashiro Chōmo (1869–1945), a student of Itosu, uses it in a hand written script. • Funakoshi and Hanashiro start a public demonstration tour across Okinawa.
1906	• Asato Ankō dies. • Funakoshi Yoshitaka is born. Yoshitaka is Gichin's third son. • Uemura Tsunejirō is born. Uemura belonged to the four main teachers at the Shōtōkan.
1907	• Hayashi Yoshiaki is born. Hayashi belonged to the four main teachers at the Shōtōkan.
1908	• Itosu writes down his text "The Chinese Hand".
1910	• Funakoshi retires from his career as a school teacher.
1911	• Funakoshi, Yabu Kentsū (1866–1937), a student of Itosu, etc. perform *kata* at a "karate festival" organized by Okinawa prefecture's normal school.

1912	• The "Okinawan Association of the Esteemed Fighting Art" (Okinawa Shōbukai) is established. Funakoshi is its chairman. • Egami Shigeru is born.
1914	• Funakoshi publishes a three-part interview with Asato ("The Martial Techniques of Okinawa"). The interview itself probably took place already in 1902.
1915	• Itosu Ankō dies.
1916	• Funakoshi demonstrates karate at the Butoku-den in Kyōto.
1918	• In the home of Mabuni Kenwa (1889–1952), a student of Itosu, the "Research Association of the Chinese hand" (Karate Kenkyūkai) is established. Funakoshi is one of its members.
1919	• Funakoshi becomes teacher (*shihan*) of karate at Okinawa prefecture's normal school.
1921	• The subsequent emperor Hirohito (1901–1989) visits Okinawa and watches a karate performance. Funakoshi is in charge of this performance.
1922	• Funakoshi introduces karate in Tōkyō and makes the Meishō-juku his headquarter there. • Funakoshi publishes his first karate book ("Ryūkyū's Fist Method: The Chinese Hand").

1924	• Funakoshi bestows his first *dan* diplomas. • The "Karate Research Association of the Privat School Keiō" is established as first karate club at a Japanese university in Tōkyō. Funakoshi is its teacher (*shihan*).
1925	• Funakoshi publishes his second karate book ("Tempering & Self Protection: Karate-Jutsu").
1926	• The denotations shuri-te, naha-te and tomari-te are created as counterproposals to the term "Chinese hand" in Okinawa. • The "Karate Research Association of the Tōkyō Imperial University" starts its regular practise. Funakoshi is its teacher (*shihan*).
1928	• Funakoshi demonstrates karate at the Saineikan within the borders of the imperial palace.
1929	• Funakoshi gradually begins to apply the spelling 「空手」 ("empty hand") and dismisses the spelling 「唐手」 ("Chinese hand"). • Funakoshi resigns from the post of teacher of the "Karate Research Association of the Tōkyō Imperial University".

1930	• Funakoshi establishes the "Great-Japan Research Association for the Way of the Chinese Hand" (Dai Nippon Karate-dō Kenkyūkai). Previously he already used the name "Research Association for the Chinese Hand" (Karate Kenkyūkai). • The "Karate Research Association of the Takushoku University" is established in Tōkyō. • Funakoshi publishes twenty teaching maxims on karate compiled by him.
1931	• The "Karate Research Association of the Tōkyō Business College" is established. Funakoshi is its teacher. (Since 1949 this school is called "Hitotsubashi University".) • The "Karate Research Association of the First High School Waseda" is established in Tōkyō. Funakoshi is its teacher.
1933	• The Butokukai opens a branch in Okinawa Prefecture.
1934	• Shimoda Takeshi dies. • Funakoshi Yoshitaka begins to take over Shimoda's functions as teaching assistant. • The karate club of the Hōsei University is established in Tōkyō. Funakoshi Gichin is its teacher.

1935	• Funakoshi publishes his third karate book ("The Teaching Standard of Karate-dō"). • Funakoshi Yoshitaka formally banishes Ōtsuka Hironori (1892–1982), an early Japanese student of Funakoshi Gichin, from the Funakoshi group.
1936	• Funakoshi renames his research association into "Great-Japan Association of the Pine Wave for the Way of the Empty Hand" (Dai Nippon Karate-dō Shōtōkai).
1937	• Japan begins a war with China and enters World War II subsequently. • Funakoshi Yoshitaka together with the Takushoku University undertakes a Korea expedition, demonstrating karate in Seoul. • Funakoshi Gichin is introduced in the "Record upon Human Affairs of Okinawa Prefecture" published by the Asahi Newspaper Publishing Company Okinawa.
1938	• In Tōkyō the construction work for Funakoshi's first independent practice hall begins. It was given the name "Building of the Pine Wave" (Shōtōkan).
1939	• Funakoshi's practise hall is inaugurated under the name "Great-Japan Building of the Pine Wave for the Way of the Empty Hand" (Dai Nippon Karate-dō Shōtōkan).

1940	• The denotation "Karate-dō Shōtōkan-ryū" is created. • The "Karate-dō Association of the Chūō University" is established in Tōkyō. Funakoshi Yoshitaka is its teacher.
1941	• Funakoshi Yoshitaka completes the stick *kata* Matsukaze no Kon. • Ten no Kata is introduced into the Shōtōkan curriculum.
1942	• A new Butokukai is established, which is a governmental organization now. Its predecessor was dissolved shortly before. • The Shōtōkai does not participate in the Butokukai.
1943	• Funakoshi publishes his fourth karate book ("Introduction into Karate").
1945	• Funakoshi Gichin moves to the island of Kyūshū. • The Shōtōkan burns as a result of an American bombing raid on Tōkyō. • Japan belongs to the losers of World War II. • Funakoshi Yoshitaka dies.
1946	• The Butokukai is dissolved.
1947	• Funakoshi Gichin returns to Tōkyō. • In Tōkyō several university karate clubs conduct a joint "welcome performance" on the occasion of Funakoshi's return.

1949	• Students of Funakoshi establish the Japan Karate Association (*Nihon Karate Kyōkai*, JKA). They appoint Funakoshi to the "highest teacher" (*saikō-shihan*) respectively the "highest technical advisor" (*saikō gijutsu komon*) of this association.
1952	• American aviators of the Strategic Air Command (SAC) shall become "combative measures instructors". For that purpose they learn particularly jūdō, however, also karate among others in Tōkyō. Funakoshi and a few of his students direct the karate lessons.
1953	• Performance on the occasion of Funakoshi's move to Tōkyō thirty years ago.
1956	• Funakoshi resigns from the post of the "highest teacher" respectively the "highest technical advisor" of the JKA. • Funakoshi publishes his fifth karate book ("The One Path of Karate-dō"). • Togawa Yukio (1912–2004), a student of both Funakoshis, includes biographies of Gichin and Yoshitaka in his work "Biographies of Fighting Arts Masters".
1957	• Funakoshi Gichin dies.
1968	• In Kamakura a memorial stone for Funakoshi Gichin is erected.

Bibliography

Japanese Sources

1 - Funakoshi, Gichin: *Karate-Dō Ichirō* (*The One Path of Karate-dō*), Tōkyō 1976

2 - Funakoshi, Gichin: *Karate-Dō Kyōhan* (*The Teaching Standard of Karate-dō*), Tōkyō 1935

3 - Funakoshi, Gichin: *Ryūkyū Kenpō. Karate* (*Ryūkyū's Fist Method: The Chinese Hand*) (commented reprint), Ginowan 1994

4 - Gima, Shinkin / Fujiwara, Ryōzō: *Kindai Karate-dō no Rekishi o kataru* (*Talking on the History of Nowadays Karate-dō*), Tōkyō 1986

5 - Hironishi, Motonobu (Edit.): *Funakoshi Gichin Sensei Karate Hondo Karate Fukyū Nanajūnen Kinen* (*Memory on Master Funakoshi Gichin's Karate Diffusion on the Main Island Seventy Years Ago*), Tōkyō 1992

6 - Hironishi, Motonobu (Edit.): *Shōtōkan Gojūnen no Ayumi* (*The Fifty Year Walk of the Shōtōkan*), Tōkyō 1988

7 - Keiō Gijuku Taiikukai Karatebu (Edit.): *Keiō Gijuku Taiikukai Karatebu Nanajūgo-Nen Shi* (*The 75 Year History of the Karate Club of the Association for Physical Education of the Private School Keiō*), Tōkyō 1999

8 - Kinjō, Hiroshi (Edit.): *Gekkan Karate-Dō. Gappon Fukkokuban* (*Karate-dō. Monthly Edition. Bound Reprint*), Ginowan 1997

9 - Kinjō, Hiroshi: *Karate kara Karate e* (*From the Chinese Hand to the Empty Hand*), Tōkyō 2011

10 - Okinawa Asahi Shinbun-Sha (Edit.): *Okinawa-ken Jinji-roku* (*Record upon Human Affairs of Okinawa Prefecture*), Naha 1937

11 - Takagi, Jōtarō (Edit.): *Shōtōkan Rokujūnen no Ayumi* (*The Sixty Year Walk of the Shōtōkan*), Tōkyō 1998

12 - Takamiyagi, Shigeru / Shinzato, Katsuhiko / Nakamoto, Masahiro (Edit.): *Okinawa Karate Kobudō Jiten* (*Encyclopedia of Okinawan Karate and Kobudō*), Tōkyō 2008

13 - Tanaka, Akira (Edit.): *Karate-dō* (*The Way of the Empty Hand*), Tōkyō 1977

14 - Togawa, Yukio: *Bugō Retsuden* (*Biographies of Fighting Arts Masters*), Tōkyō 1956

(Internet)

15 - http://www.sendaihira.jp/yurai.html

Western Sources

16 - Bowring, Richard / Kornicki, Peter (Edit.): *The Cambridge Encyclopedia of Japan*, New York 1993

17 - Corcoran, John / Farkas, Emil: *The Original Martial Arts Encyclopedia. Tradition, History, Pioneers*, Los Angeles 1993

18 - Kerr, George: *Okinawa – The History of an Island People* (Revised Edition), Tōkyō 2000

19 - Wittwer, Henning: *Shōtōkan - überlieferte Texte & historische Untersuchungen* (Band I), Niesky 2007

20 - Wittwer, Henning: *Shōtōkan - überlieferte Texte & historische Untersuchungen. Band II*, Niesky 2012

Sources of Figures

"*Gekkan Karate-dō*" (8): p. 89 / 93
"*Karate-dō*" (13): p. 74 / 77
"*Karate-dō Kyōhan*" (2): p. 82 / 84
"*Keiō Gijuku*" (7): p. 76 / 91
"*Martial Arts Encyclopedia*" (17): p. 90
Shōtōkai: p. 12 / 73 / 75 / 78 / 79 / 80 / 81 / 83 /
85 / 86 / 87 / 88 / 92 / 94
Henning Wittwer: p. 95

About the Author

Henning Wittwer took up his karate practise in
1992. From the beginning he followed the
Shōtōkan current, initially in the more sport and
tournament orientated organisations. Since 2005
he published his translations of old Japanese
sources and his research regarding karate in
German as well as in English journals and
magazines. Wittwer is the author of the German
books *Shōtōkan - überlieferte Texte & historische
Untersuchungen* (*Shōtōkan – Transmitted Texts &
Historical Research*) (2007), *Shōtōkan –
überlieferte Texte & historische Untersuchungen.
Band II* (*Shōtōkan – Transmitted Texts &
Historical Research. Vol. II*) (2012), *Funakoshi
Gichin & Funakoshi Yoshitaka - Zwei Karate-
Meister* (*Funakoshi Gichin & Funakoshi Yoshitaka -
Two Karate Masters*) (2013), and *Karate.
Kampfkunst. Hoplologie* (*Karate. Fighting Art.
Hoplology*) (2014).

He can be contacted at: www.gibukai.de

»Scouting Out The Historical Course Of Karate: Collected Essays«
By Henning Wittwer

The six essays in this book are primarily based on Japanese sources and the original research of the author. Each of them provides valuable and unique insights into the history and teachings of the martial art of the Ryūkyū Kingdom, today widely known as karate.

Henning Wittwer takes a deep look at the following themes:

• The 1867 „Programme of the Three-Six-Nine and of All Arts": A New Translation and Explanation of its Martial Arts Sections

• Asato Ankō – His Life, Teachings, & Descendants

• Bodhidharma, Shaolin and Chinese Boxing in the Eyes of Japan's Karate Pioneers

• Jigen-ryū & its Influence upon Karate-Dō

• The Karate of the Shōtōkan (1938–1945)

• The Stick of the Shōtōkan – Considerations Concerning its History, Transmission and Teachings

Karate practitioners, karate researchers, and martial arts enthusiasts, students of Japanese Studies and people with a general interest in Asian history and culture will find this book fascinating as well as interesting.

Paperback, 164 pages
Book Dimensions: 5.8 x 0.4 x 8.3 inches
ISBN: 978-1291662658

Available directly at lulu.com

28520539R00063

Made in the USA
San Bernardino, CA
30 December 2015